Foreword

IN THIS BOOK, WILLIAM MacQUITTY PRESENTS A SERIES OF PHOTOGRAPHS of unusual and striking character which evoke the mystery of Ancient Egypt, through to the death and burial of Tutankhamun. It is not easy to get close to the Egypt of the fourteenth century B.C., to understand the ways of thought which produced the remarkable culture of that time, to comprehend truly the emotions and aspirations which pervade the strange burial customs practised by the Ancient Egyptians. We can read the ancient texts inscribed in the tombs of the great kings, but we can scarcely fathom what they mean. As the mature statements of a royal religion, they were put up in a tomb for the personal use of the dead king, to assist him in the long and hazardous, but inevitably successful, journey to join his father, the sun god Re, in the glorious after-life. It may be doubted whether any Egyptian himself would have understood what they meant. But they were part of the essential ritual of death and burial.

The small tomb prepared for Tutankhamun was only modestly provided with the wall-paintings which in most royal tombs incorporated the texts. This deficiency was largely compensated for by the inclusion of four gilded shrines surrounding the sarcophagus of the king. These shrines were covered, inside and out, with religious inscriptions of baffling content. The photographs in this volume illustrate the strange, arcane creatures which people the scenes that accompany these inscriptions.

It is 150 years since the French scholar, Jean-François Champollion published the discoveries which led directly to the decipherment of Egyptian hieroglyphs. In the intervening years since 1822 much has been learned about Egypt. Yet whoever gazes on the objects found there will still sense the mystery embodied in peculiar ritual objects and images of strange divine creatures, and wonder at the technical and artistic achievement of the ancient craftsmen.

William MacQuitty's evocative photographs and text offer a sensitive presentation of the life and death of Tutankhamun, illuminated by illustrations which convey the drama surrounding the burial of the king and the excitement of the discovery of the tomb fifty years ago.

Left: An effigy of Tutankhamun made of wood covered with painted plaster.

T. G. H. James
Assistant Keeper of the Department of Egyptian Antiquities,
British Museum, London

WILLIAM MACQUITTY IS AN HONORARY M.A. OF THE QUEEN'S University, Belfast, a Fellow of the Royal Geographical Society, a Fellow of the Royal Photographic Society and the producer of such films as *A Night to Remember* about the sinking of the Titanic.

His books: *Abu Simbel, Buddha, Great Botanical Gardens of the World, Princes of Jade,* and *The World in Focus* have won him international renown and he has been widely praised for his sensitivity as an artist. Henry Moore said of *Abu Simbel*: 'This book is a fitting and beautiful memorial which vividly records the statues for the last time in their original setting.' He was chosen by His Imperial Majesty, the Shah of Iran, from photographers from all over the world for the book *Persia, The Immortal Kingdom,* the commemorative volume for the 2,500th anniversary of the founding of the Kingdom of Persia by Cyrus the Great.

His latest book *Island of Isis* describes the temple of Philae, the most beautiful temple of Ancient Egypt, which is being saved from inundation by funds raised internationally through UNESCO and by proceeds from the exhibitions of the Treasures of Tutankhamun.

His picture of the gold funerary mask of Tutankhamun was *The Times* official poster for the exhibition of the Treasures of Tutankhamun at the British Museum, London.

Overleaf: The second mummiform coffin shows Tutankhamun wearing a sad expression in contrast to the serenity of the funeral mask. It is made of wood covered with sheets of beaten gold inlaid with semi-precious stones.

TUTANKHAMUN
The Last Journey

TEXT AND PHOTOGRAPHS BY
WILLIAM MacQUITTY

A Quartet book,
distributed by Crown Publishers, Inc.,
One Park Avenue, New York, N.Y. 10016

Library of Congress Cataloging in Publishing Data

MacQuitty, William
Tutankhamun, The Last Journey
LCN 76-286-58

ISBN 0-517-531704
ISBN 0-517-531712 pbk.

Acknowledgements

I wish to thank Mr T. G. H. James, Keeper of Egyptian Antiquities of the
British Museum who most kindly wrote the Foreword and checked my
manuscript. Mr James was instrumental in bringing the treasure of
Tutankhamun to London for exhibition at the British Museum and also
provided material for the design of the commemorative stamp issued to
mark the fiftieth anniversary of the opening of the tomb.

I owe special thanks to my many friends in Egypt; my deepest gratitude
to H. E. Dr Abd el-Qadir Hatem, formerly Deputy Prime Minister and
Minister of Information and Culture, H. E. Dr Gamal ed-Din Mukhtar,
Under-Secretary of State in charge of the Antiquities Service, and Dr Henry
Riad, formerly Chief Keeper of the Cairo Museum, who enabled me to
photograph the great collections under his charge. Warm thanks are due to
H. E. Adel Taher, Under-Secretary of State in the Ministry of Tourism, and
to the many members of his department who helped me in my travels.
Lastly I would like to express my appreciation to the people of Egypt, who
were invariably kind and courteous.

Technical Data

Cameras:	two Nikon F Photomic Tn, one Nikkormat FT.
Lenses:	Nikkor Auto 20 mm $f/3\cdot5$, 28 mm $f/3\cdot5$, 35 mm $f/2\cdot8$, 55 mm $f/3\cdot5$, 105 mm $f/2\cdot5$, 200 mm $f/4\cdot0$. All with lens hoods and skylight filters.
Film stock:	Kodachrome II given normal exposure at meter readings with shutter speeds of 1/125th of a second or faster.
Flash:	three lightweight Mecablitz with mains charging units.

Cover designed by Mike Jarvis, text designed by Craig Dodd
Photographs copyright MacQuitty International Collection, London, NW74HH

Printed in the U.S.A.
Third Printing, March, 1978

Left: Servant offering perfume to ladies. Tomb of Nakht, Eighteenth Dynasty.

Below: Hunting and fishing in the marshes. A scene from the tomb of Menna, a scribe. The walls of royal tombs were not decorated with scenes of everyday life and it is only from private tombs that we can learn anything about the pleasures of the court and the non-warlike activities of the king. Luxor Eighteenth Dynasty, c. 1420 B.C.

Overleaf: Tutankhamun in his war-chariot attacking the Syrians. Painted on the stuccoed side of a wooden chest.

daughter, Lady Evelyn Herbert, his devoted companion in all his Egyptian explorations.

On the 24th the stairway to the door was completely cleared and it was possible to make out the name Tutankhamun on several of the seals. But now that the whole door was exposed to light it became all too clear that it had been broken into twice and twice resealed by the inspectors of the necropolis. Beyond the door a rubble-filled passage continued for 30 ft. In the middle of the afternoon of the 26th, the passage was cleared to reveal a second sealed door bearing signs of having been opened and resealed in a similar manner to the first. With trembling hands Carter made a tiny breach in the upper left-hand corner. At first the escaping air caused the candle to flicker, 'but presently, as my eyes grew accustomed to the light, details of the room within emerged slowly from the mist, strange animals, statues, and gold – everywhere the glint of gold. For the moment – an eternity it must have seemed to the others standing by – I was struck dumb with amazement, and when Lord Carnarvon, unable to stand the suspense any longer enquired anxiously, "Can you see anything?", it was all I could do to get out the words "Yes, wonderful things."' Quickly the opening was enlarged and the gloomy interior revealed a strange jumble of animals, statues, boxes, the furnishings of death left in total confusion by the plunderers, but nevertheless the most complete evidence of the royal funeral cult of Ancient Egypt ever to be found.

The tomb contained four rooms. The antechamber entered from the

passage, beyond it on the left side of the facing wall a small store room and on the right wall the entrance to the burial chamber, which had an opening to the innermost treasury, on its right wall. The antechamber was 26 ft by 12 ft, the annex 13 ft by 10 ft, the burial chamber 21 ft by 13 ft and the treasury 13 ft by 11 ft. In these four tiny rooms lay the greatest collection of treasures the world has ever known, or rather what was left of them, because Carter was of the opinion that a great deal of the most valuable contents, with the exception of the sarcophagus and its shrines, had been stolen. Twice thieves had broken in and in their haste scattered and overturned the precisely arranged funeral objects, searching in the stifling atmosphere with flickering torches for the most precious articles. Twice the inspectors of the necropolis had entered the tomb and endeavoured to set things to rights, twice they had resealed the doors, but their efforts were half-hearted and the confusion that greeted Carter and Carnarvon must have been extremely distressing. Miraculously out of the welter came the richest archaeological find known to history, for although the thieves had entered the burial chamber the huge gilded shrine of wood which filled the room appeared to be intact. The robbers may have thought it too formidable to tackle; it stood 9 ft high and was almost 11 ft wide and 16½ ft long – all but filling the chamber. In the flickering light the side may have looked like a solid wall. Perhaps they were surprised in their theft and had to escape, or they may have decided to complete their work later; fortunately they never returned and the benefit for posterity was incalculable.

Below: The menacing head of a hippopotamus guards a funeral bed in the tomb of Tutankhamun.

Right: Detail from the head of one of the ritual beds shows a cow goddess made of gilded wood.

Overleaf: A village on the Nile near Luxor, very similar to those in the days of Tutankhamun.

Left: Amon-Re, Lord of Heaven, Chief of the gods – the composite form of Amun and Re.

Below: The sanctuary area of the Temple of Karnak. In the background are two square pillars decorated with the papyrus and lily, symbolising Lower and Upper Egypt.

Overleaf: The avenue of ram-headed Sphinxes leading to the great Temple of Karnak where Tutankhamun had a sanctuary.

As Carter and Carnarvon came to examine the doors of the shrine they were dismayed to find that in spite of first appearances the stamped clay seals were broken, showing that the gilded doors had been opened after the closing of the tomb. But beneath the first shrine lay a second covered with a cloth decorated with bronze daisies, and its doors still bore unbroken seals. Obviously it had not been opened since the burial 3,274 years ago. The excitement was intense: for the first time in history the mummy of a Pharaoh with all its sacred trappings was preserved absolutely intact for the archaeologists.

Within the second shrine was a third, its seals intact, and within it a fourth, also of gilded wood. Like a fairy story the fourth shrine was removed to reveal a magnificent quartzite sarcophagus carved from a single block of stone 9 ft long by almost 5 ft in width and height inscribed with the king's name. The rose granite lid broken in two across the middle had been cemented together and tinted to match the rest of the stone. At each corner the guardian goddesses, Isis, Nephthys, Neith and Selkis were beautifully carved in high relief, their outstretched arms and wings clasping the sarcophagus in their protective embrace.

The lifting of the lid was another dramatic experience in the lives of the archaeologists; for the first time the burial customs for a Pharaoh dead for nearly thirty-three centuries were to be revealed. The heavy cover, weighing over a ton, rose slowly with the tackles exposing disappointingly drab linen shrouds. When they were removed an astonishing sight appeared –

the gorgeous effigy of the young king wrought in sheet gold, multi-coloured stones and glass. This was the lid of a mummiform coffin, 7 ft long, resting on a low bier in the form of a lion. The sculpture of the face and hands was superb – a lifelike portrait. On his brow sat the vulture and the serpent, their outlines inlaid with red and blue glass. The king's hands were folded on his chest, the left hand holding the crook rested under the right which held the flail. These royal emblems of Osiris were also inlaid with coloured glass and semi-precious stones. Within this splendid sheath was yet another made of wood like the first, covered with sheets of gold similarly inlaid. The face on this coffin wears a look of suffering – the sadness of death in youth. Within the second coffin lay a third wrapped in a red linen shroud. The coffins fitted so snugly into each other that there was less than half an inch separating them, but this provided sufficient space for little wreaths of flowers to be laid between: blue lotuses, olive leaves and willow, still faintly showing traces of their original colour, simple reminders that the Ancient Egyptians were not so far removed from ourselves.

The greatest surprise was yet to come – the innermost coffin was not fashioned of beaten gold laid on a wood base like the first two. To the

Right: The sun sets across the Nile behind the Valley of the Kings where the mummy of Tutankhamun still rests in his gold outermost coffin.

Set: A malevolent, violent god, the brother and slayer of Osiris. A particularly prominent deity during the Nineteenth Dynasty. He is shown with the head of an animal that has not been satisfactorily identified; perhaps a pig or the okapi.

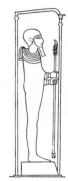

Ptah: The great god of Memphis and one of the most important of gods throughout Egyptian history. The great creator god, he was regarded as the patron of artists and craftsmen. He was represented as a human, mummiform, on a statue base, often placed within a kiosk or shrine.

Left: The obelisk of Queen Hatshepsut at Karnak Temple. To the left is the lily column of Tuthmosis III, showing the king being embraced by the goddess Mut.

Overleaf: Priests carry the sacred bark of Amun. Wall-carving on the Temple of Karnak.

Left: These seated figures of Amenophis III, father of Akhenaten, known as the Colossi of Memnon, were passed by the funeral procession of Tutankhamun on its way to the Valley of the Kings. Luxor Eighteenth Dynasty, c. *1420* B.C.

Below: Mourners in the tomb of Ramose, governor of Thebes during the reign of Akhenaten. He was one of the earliest converts to the new faith established by the Pharaoh who decreed that there should only be one god, the sun.

astonishment of the archaeologists and the world it was found to be solid 22-carat gold weighing an incredible 296 lb troy, the equivalent of 110.4 kg.

The face on the third coffin was calm and reposed. The nemes head-dress was plain gold and not inset with bars of colour like the others. The eyes had lost their look of anguish and the expression was tranquil and profoundly moving. The sacred goddesses of Upper and Lower Egypt, Nekhbet, the vulture and Wadjet, the serpent, rested on the king's brow and their colour stood out vividly against the plain gold. As in the other coffins they also appeared on the arms of the king, the vulture on the right arm and the serpent (with vulture body) on the left. Protectively embracing the gold body of the king were the interlaced wings of the goddesses Isis and Nephthys.

All the coffins were fashioned to represent Osiris, the god of the dead who was closer to man than any of the other gods. His story bears some resemblance to that of Christ. While he was sovereign of Egypt he travelled about the country winning the minds of men by wisdom rather than by force. His brother Set was jealous of him and conspired to kill him. This he eventually succeeded in doing with the help of confederates and threw the corpse into the Nile. Isis, his wife, recovered the body and Re, the sun god sent down his son Anubis to wrap it in bandages like those of a mummy. Isis beat her wings and caused breath to enter into it and Osiris moved and

lived again. Unable to return to his former life as an earthly king, he ruled in the spirit world and became god of the dead. In this position he did not conflict with any of the living gods, and no Egyptian, whatever his town god, had any difficulty in also adopting Osiris and his creed. This was essentially that man lived again in the underworld after death, provided the proper rites were observed. Every Egyptian believed that because Osiris died and rose again to live in eternal blessedness he, too, could achieve the same destiny, provided that the requirements of religion had been duly satisfied and that he became one with Osiris.

So eventually Carter, after removing four shrines, two linen covers, a stone sarcophagus, three shrouds and three nesting mummiform coffins, came to the royal mummy. Unhappily his patron, Lord Carnarvon, was not to witness this final triumph. In March 1923 he was bitten by a mosquito; the bite turned septic and as the infection spread he decided to return to Cairo. Here the infection was cleared up but he contracted pneumonia from which he died on 5 April 1923. His death was later followed by two more connected with the discovery, namely Georges Bénédite, head of the Department of Egyptian Antiquities at the Louvre in 1926, and Arthur C. Mace, another member of the excavation team, in 1928. The sensation-loving public saw the 'Mummy's curse' in these natural events and failed to appreciate that Howard Carter and his many distinguished colleagues who photographed, tabulated and analysed the mummy all remained alive although they were more deeply involved.

Below: The Valley of the Kings at Luxor, showing the debris from other tombs which concealed the entrance to the tomb of Tutankhamun for over thirty-two centuries.

Isis: The divine embodiment of motherhood, wife of Osiris and mother of Horus. She was a mourning deity and one of the four goddesses who protected the dead body. In a different tradition she was also a goddess of magic and guile. During the last centuries of antiquity her great cult centre was on the Island of Philae.

Osiris: According to tradition an early king of Egypt who was martyred and became the deity of the underworld. At first the king in death was identified with him; later all dead people hoped for this identification. He was also a god of fertility and growing crops. He was shown as a mummified king. There were Osiris shrines throughout Egypt, the principal one being at Abydos.

Right: Plan of Tutankhamun's tomb.

Overleaf: The goddess Nephthys whose winged arm protectively embraces the second gilt shrine, one of the four which encased the stone sarcophagus of Tutankhamun.

One of the treasures that Lord Carnarvon was not to see was the finest funerary mask ever discovered and the most important object in the magnificent treasure of the tomb. The mask fitted closely over the king's head and was a faithful portrait of natural size. It weighed 22 lb, a little less than 10 kg, and was of solid gold beaten and burnished. The stripes of the nemes head-dress were made of blue glass; the eyes, which are particularly striking, are made of quartz and obsidian with the eyelids and eyebrows picked out in lapis lazuli. On the chest was a broad collar encrusted with lapis lazuli, quartz and green felspar with a lotus-bud border and each side of the collar ended in a falcon's head of gold. The vulture upon the brow was made of solid gold as was also the cobra, whose head was covered with dark blue faience, the hood inlaid with lapis lazuli and carnelian, gold cloisonné inlaid with translucent quartz backed with a red pigment forming the eyes. The portrait resembled Akhenaten, his father-in-law and also Queen Tiye, Akhenaten's mother; perhaps one day further discoveries will reveal the parents of this young king. It is interesting that although Egypt was a land of gold and many precious things, diamonds, rubies, sapphires and pearls were unknown at this time.

Beneath the mask the mummy was swathed in yards of fine linen bandages which covered it from head to foot. As the bandages were removed they revealed 143 gold and jewelled ornaments distributed about the body, charms and amulets for the protection of the king in the underworld. The king's hands and feet were uncovered, each finger and toe protected by a

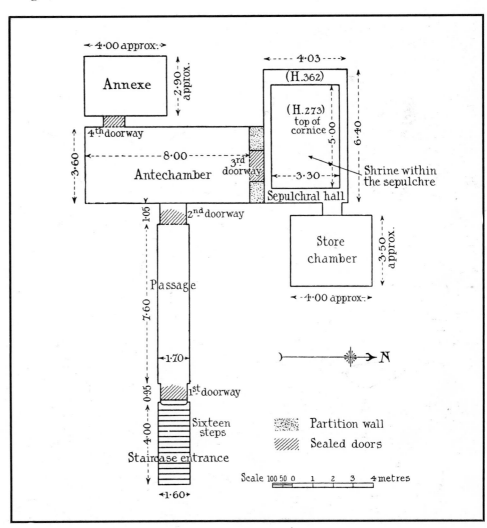

stall of gold. The royal penis had been bandaged in a state of erection and a fine linen skull-cap covered the head, beneath which, unlike all the other royal mummies, there was no hair, for it had been shaved off by the embalmers.

The operation of embalming in its most developed form took a specific period of seventy days to perform and the result was almost always permanent. Embalming was a highly skilled profession, involving the skills of surgeon and priest. Arriving at the house of the dead person, the embalmers would set up a tent containing a table on which the body was laid. It is probable in the case of Tutankhamun that this was performed at his palace at Malkata on the west bank of the Nile at Thebes (Luxor), although some embalming materials were found near his tomb. Mummification was an essential part of the religion of Ancient Egypt, for without a body there could be no resurrection; for eternal life it was a practical necessity. No worse fate could befall a king or any person of importance than that his mummy should be destroyed or lost, hence the elaborate precautions that were taken to ensure its safety, alas as we have seen, of little avail in a world of greed. The object was to render the body incorruptible so that it became divine and could arise again like the sun in the morning and achieve eternal life.

Embalming was also practised by the Israelites when they were in Egypt, according to Genesis, chapter 50, verses 2 and 3. 'Joseph commanded his servants the physicians to embalm his father . . . and forty days were fulfilled . . . the days of those who are embalmed . . . and the Egyptians mourned him for three score days and ten.'

The method was quite straightforward and there are many examples of its effectiveness. The mummies of Seti I and Ramesses I and many others

Right: The goddess Selkis guards the gilded shrine containing the four canopic jars holding the viscera of Tutankhamun.

Below: Carter's first glimpse of the antechamber (26 November 1922). 'Wonderful things' . . .

Left: Looking down on the representation of Tutankhamun on the lid of his second mummiform coffin.

Min: A very ancient god whose worship was based on the town of Coptos. A god of fertility he was later often associated with the Theban deity Amun. He was usually shown as a mummiform figure on a statue base, with one arm raised holding the royal symbol, the flagellum, and with erect penis. Behind him stands a formal garden planted with bolting lettuces, a further sign of fertility.

Overleaf: The tomb of Tutankhamun, as it probably looked in the red glow of the torches when the royal burial took place in 1352 B.C. The outermost mummiform coffin, which can be seen lying in the great quartzite sarcophagus, still contains the mummy of the king. Behind the sarcophagus are wall-paintings of the rituals of death.

reveal the characters of the living men with much more impact than their rather stylised statues. First the corpse was washed with water from the Nile, next a slit was cut in the left side with a flint knife and all the organs removed with the exception of the heart, which would be required by the body when it came to face judgement before Osiris and the forty-two terrible assessors – then it would be weighed in the balance against truth. The organs, being more perishable, were placed in four urns, known as 'canopic jars', and were protected by the addition of natron and aromatic spices. In the case of Tutankhamun an additional refinement was the bandaging of the mummified organs and placing them in tiny replicas of the large coffins before putting them in the canopic jars. The contents of the jars were guarded by their respective goddesses: Isis guarded the liver, Nephthys the lungs, Neith the stomach and Selkis the intestines. In the tomb these jars were found in the store chamber which opened directly to the burial chamber, having no door between, presumably so that the vital organs could the more easily be reunited to their body when needed. The jars, capped with fine alabaster stoppers carved with the king's head, were found in an alabaster chest placed in an elegant gilt shrine with the four goddesses standing at the four sides and holding it protectively with their outstretched arms. In front of the shrine Anubis, the jackal god of embalming, crouched menacingly lifelike. The body was made of black varnished wood, the claws were of silver and details of the eyes and ears were outlined in gold.

Now that the more perishable contents had been removed there remained the task of preserving the royal corpse. The empty body cavity was washed out with palm wine and other astringents. The brain was removed by breaking the bone at the back of the nose with a metal instrument and gradually extracting the soft tissue through the nostrils. In X-ray photographs it is possible to see the broken bone lying at the back of the skull where it has been forced by the extractor. Any residue of brain was dissolved out with cedar oil and other astringents and the cavity filled with resinous matter. After this the body was packed and covered with natron, a naturally occurring compound of sodium carbonate and sodium bicarbonate, which assisted the process of drying and acted as a preservative just as salt and saltpetre do in the curing of bacon today. Undoubtedly the extremely dry climate also helped to preserve the body; bodies of earlier inhabitants of Egypt have been recovered reasonably well preserved by the desiccating quality of the hot dry desert sand. During the seventy days of mummification the priests recited the necessary prayers and incantations which ensured the dead king a safe journey to the next world, where, thanks to the power of Osiris who died and rose again from the dead, he would obtain eternal life.

Finally, with the body cured, the last stage commenced. Many yards of fine linen were used to cover the king's body with protective layers. Bandaging began with the extremities. First the fingers then the forearms were wrapped, the folds making elegant patterns, then the upper arms with the hands folded across the chest, right over left and bound in position. In the case of the mummy of Ramesses the Great the left hand has worked loose and one may see it in the Cairo Museum raised as though in a last

defiant gesture of this remarkable Pharaoh. The dried shrunken tissues were padded out to their original dimensions with rolls of linen and the body cavities stuffed with cloth. During the bandaging the correct prayers were intoned and unguents poured on the bandages. Many varieties were used: myrrh, olive oil, cedar oil, wax, cassia, gums, aromatics and astringents. The amounts were very important, too much would eat away the flesh, too little would fail to preserve. Between the layers of bandages all manner of precious things were placed, each designed for a special purpose and carrying with it the incantations and blessings of the priests. The royal mummy was now completely swathed, the amulets and charms all in place; next it was wrapped in shrouds which were tied with four transverse bands and three running from head to foot. The high priest gave the final benediction, 'You live again you live for ever, here you are young once more for ever.'

At the royal palace at Malkata the mummification of the young Pharaoh was complete and preparations commenced for the funeral ceremony. Carefully the exquisite funerary mask was placed over the royal head. The mummy thus arrayed was lowered into the bottom half of the solid gold coffin and profusely anointed with sacred unguents; unfortunately, whatever the pious intentions, they formed a pitch-like cement which Carter found almost impossible to remove, and worse still, the acids given off by them over the years acted destructively on the mummy and its invaluable trappings. The heavy lid was now secured and the mummiform coffin placed in the second coffin and this in turn enclosed in the third and final coffin. In the slim space between these nesting coffins, less than a finger's width, little posies and wreaths of flowers were laid to remain undisturbed until the coffins were opened by Carter. The flowers served another purpose in that they were considered to be those found in the spring and would therefore suggest that the funeral took place in the early part of the year.

It is probable that on a day appointed by the Vizir Ay – who is shown on the wall of the tomb performing the Opening of the Mouth ceremony for Tutankhamun – the funeral procession started from the palace with the important priests, officials and relatives. The mummy, accompanied by the chest containing the canopic jars, may have been taken first through the vast temples of Luxor and Karnak where the young Pharaoh had dedicated buildings, monuments and inscriptions to the gods during his lifetime. All these unfortunately were later to be obliterated by his general Horemheb in his ruthless efforts to remove all traces of Tutankhamun from history – indeed the general would almost have succeeded but for the discovery of the tomb by Carter.

After the ceremonies in the temples for the living the cortège crossed the Nile for the long journey to the Valley of the Kings. The mummy was borne in the magnificent funeral bark across the milk-green water which gave the name Eau-de-Nil to the world's vocabulary. Landing on the west bank the mourners, led by the priests and nobles, followed the heavy sled carrying the coffins as it wound its way slowly past the huge statues of Amenophis III, now known as the Colossi of Memnon. A few miles further on the procession passed the beautiful Temple of Hatshepsut, the first important woman Pharaoh, before commencing the long ascent to the

Right: Ay, Tutankhamun's successor, performs the ceremony of Opening the Mouth, Eyes and Nose of the mummified king, who is shown in the guise of Osiris, so that he may live again.

Re-Herakhty: A composite god of the kind evolved by Egyptian religion to reconcile differing traditions or to effect political unions. He was a falcon god, like Horus, and a sun god, like Re. The particular form of Horus embodied in this composition was 'Horus of the Horizon', *akhty* being the Egyptian for 'of the Horizon', a reference to the eastern horizon where the sun could first be seen on rising. This god was not proscribed during the reign of Akhenaten.

Thoth: The ibis-headed god whose principal cult centre was Hermopolis; he was also sometimes shown as a baboon. He was considered to be the inventor of the hieroglyphic script and consequently the scribe of the gods.

Overleaf: Detail from the second shrine, showing deities of the underworld whom Tutankhamun would have encountered in his journey after death.

Valley of the Kings, where except for Akhenaten all the Pharaohs were buried. Akhenaten, considered by some to be the father of Tutankhamun, had elected to be buried at El-Amarna where he had built the city of Akhetaten, meaning 'The Horizon of Aten', as a centre for his new cult, the worship of one god, the solar disc. At last the cortège reached the lonely head of the valley where they halted and the heavy nesting coffins were carefully carried through the narrow entrance of a small tomb. Owing to the unexpected death of so young a king there had not been enough time to prepare one of appropriate size – this one had probably been designed for an important official, perhaps indeed for Ay himself.

In the centre of the small burial chamber stood the huge quartzite sarcophagus where it still stands today and still guards the royal mummy which rests there, in its outer coffin, the other two coffins being in the Cairo Museum. Looking at it one wonders how those ancient workers managed to move such a large and unwieldy object in the confined space. One can sympathise with their discomfiture when the huge lid, in spite of their best endeavours, cracked in two. The heavy nest of coffins was gently lowered on to the lion-shaped bed and the broken lid of the sarcophagus placed in position and cemented. Now the four gilt shrines were placed round the sarcophagus, one encasing the other – the doors of each one being sealed in turn by the priests. The household treasures of Tutankhamun were placed in the chambers of the tomb in their designated positions. Many were kept in their boxes, including the Ushabti-figures or 'answerers' – little Osiride statuettes which could be magically animated

Above: Nobles drawing the sled bearing the mummy of Tutankhamun. Painting on the east wall of his tomb.

Bastet: The chief deity of the Delta city known as Bubastis by the Greeks (in Egyptian the name meant 'Town of Bastet'). A cat goddess, she was generally considered a kindly deity. During later periods her worship became more generally popular, and her festival at Bubastis an annual event of great moment, attended by vast crowds of pilgrims intent on enjoying all the 'fun of the fair' which accompanied the solemn ceremonies of worship and procession.

Khnum: A ram-headed deity who was thought to have been the god who actually fashioned the body and soul of man like a potter working on his wheel. As such he is shown in the formal representations illustrating the divine birth of the Egyptian king in the temples of Luxor and Deir el-Bahri. He was also the principal god of the First Cataract region, the centre of his cult being on the Island of Elephantine.

in the hereafter to work for their master. Chapter Six of the Book of the Dead reads, 'Oh thou, this Ushabti, if thou art commanded to do what has to be done in the nether world of various kinds of work, then say "Here I am."' Sometimes, perhaps to avoid the possibility of quarrelling, there were separate Ushabti-figures for each day of the year. Later in the history of Ancient Egypt even more were added, as many as 700, so many that they had to be divided into groups with their own special implements and foremen with whips to control them. Written on the wall of a tomb was occasionally a warning notice, 'Obey only him who made thee' – an admonition to prevent them from working for someone else.

Gradually the strange mixture of thrones, chariots, animal-shaped beds, walking-sticks, weapons, games, ornaments, perfumes, statues, guardian figures and gods were all assembled in their appointed places. Perhaps the most moving objects were the tiny coffins containing the bodies of presumably his two stillborn children who might have continued the line. At last all was done – the priests withdrew and the masons closed the entrance of the tomb.

After the mourning came the banquet with dancing and singing, music and feasting. Near its end perhaps the blind harper sang as he still sings on the wall of a tomb:

'Rejoice and let thy heart forget that day when they shall lay thee to rest.
Cast all sorrow behind thee, and bethink thee of joy until there come that
    day of reaching port in the land that loveth silence.

Follow thy desire as long as thou livest, put myrrh on thy head, clothe
thee in fine linen.
Set singing and music before thy face.
Increase yet more the delights which thou hast, and let not thy heart
grow weary.
Spend a happy day and weary not thereof. Lo none may take his goods
with him, and none that have gone may come again.'

Thus ended the final chapter in the history of Tutankhamun, but there
is a mention of his widow Ankhesenamun; she in her loneliness is said to
have sent a letter to the Hittite king Shuppiluliumash saying that her
husband had died leaving her no son and asking him to send one of his
sons to marry her. After a further exchange of letters to reassure Shuppiluliumash, who thought it might be a trap, she confirmed that his son
would be made king in Egypt. The monarch sent his son Zannanzash, but
unfortunately the poor man was murdered before he reached his destina-
tion, and here, too, the pages of history close for the young queen and her
fate remains a mystery.

Tutankhamun achieved more in his death than he ever did while he was
alive. Little is known about the boy-king and there are many conjectures
about his parentage. Some think that he was a brother of Smenkhkare and
that they were the children of Amenophis III and his wife Tiye. This has
been strengthened by an X-ray examination carried out when the mummy
was taken out of its coffin in 1968. Certainly they both married daughters
of Akhenaten which helped them to become Pharaohs, if only briefly.
Behind the royal family stood two powerful men: Ay the Vizir and
Horemheb, the general in command of the army – a man of tradition,
contemptuous of Aten and the new religion. Both of them were to become
Pharaohs in their turn.

Tutankhaten, 'Living Image of Aten', as Tutankhamun was called for the
first twelve years of his life, was, with the exception of Ay, the last of
the line to be involved in the religion of Aten. He replaced Smenkhkare,
who had a brief and ephemeral reign at the city of Akhetaten, built with
such high hopes by Akhenaten as the centre for his new cult but destined
to dwindle into obscurity. For some years Tutankhaten continued to
worship Aten, but at the same time he began to come to terms with the
priesthood of Amun. Things were not going well with the kingdom. The
policies of love and kindness with which the liberal and spiritually minded
Akhenaten governed had little of the force or cunning needed to hold his
enemies in check. He had overthrown the old gods Amun and Osiris, the
protectors and friends of the people, and had abolished all the magical
paraphernalia that was to give them advantages over the powers of darkness. Such a decree of the State had no more effect on his subjects than
a similar decree of Theodosius had when he banished the old gods of Egypt
in favour of Christianity. Worship of the old gods continued.

In 1362 Akhenaten died. After his death he was known as 'That criminal
of Akhetaten [El-Amarna]', but posterity will remember him as the world's
first idealist who undaunted by age-old tradition bravely gave a new con-
cept of love and duty to his people that was far above the ability of his age

*Right: Ushabti figures who
would by magical animation
work for the dead king in the
hereafter.*

Maat: A goddess of importance
throughout Egyptian history, she
embodied truth, order in nature, in
a sense the golden mean. She was
shown as a woman with an ostrich
feather on her head, and the feather
alone often represented her, as in
scenes of judgement when the
feather is set against the heart (soul)
in the pans of the balances of Thoth.
During the reign of Akhenaten,
Maat assumed special importance as
the divine element of order given by
the Aten to the world.

Amon-Re: The god of the
Egyptian Empire, a composite deity
uniting the characteristics of Amun
'the hidden one', the god of Thebes,
and Re, the sun god. The great
temples at Karnak and Luxor were
devoted to his cult, and with their
resident priesthoods received much
of the tribute derived from foreign
conquests. Because of the power and
fateful influence of the god and his
followers, his worship was
proscribed in the reign of
Akhenaten, but fully restored under
Tutankhamun.

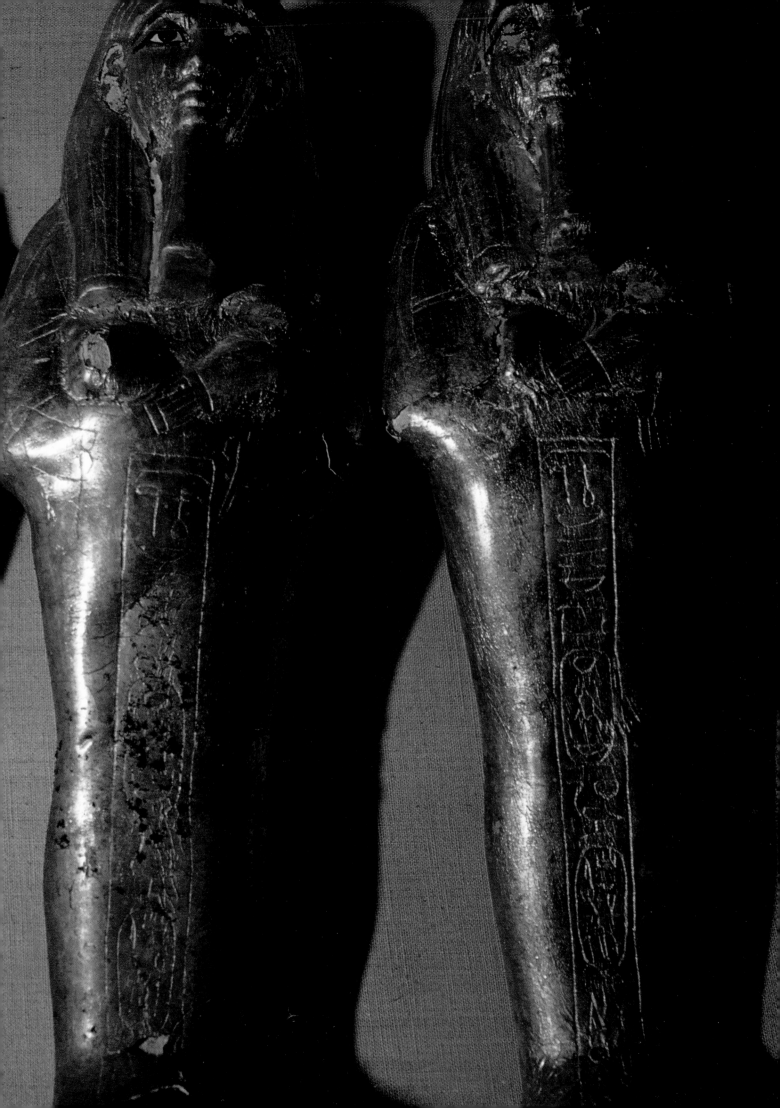

to understand Like the great Indian monarch Ashoka who lived a thousand years later, he shone forth a bright and lonely star among the arrogance of the all-powerful god-kings of Egypt.

After the death of Akhenaten, the boy-king was under increasing pressure from the priests to restore the old religion, and one of his first acts was to erect a large stele near the Third Pylon in the huge Temple of Karnak, showing him making offerings to Amun and carrying the following inscription:

'When His Majesty arose as king, the temples of the gods and goddesses, beginning from Elephantine down to the marshes of the Delta had fallen into decay, their shrines had fallen into desolation and become ruins overgrown with weeds, their chapels as though they had never been and their halls serving as footpaths. The land was topsy-turvy and the gods turned their backs on this land. If messengers were sent to Djahi [Syria] to extend the boundaries of Egypt, they had no success. If one humbled oneself to a god to ask a thing from him, he did not come, and if prayer was made to a goddess, likewise she never came. . . . But after many days My Majesty arose from the seat of his father and ruled over the territories of Horus, the Black Land and the Red Land being under his supervision.'

Egypt of the Pharaohs, Gardiner, pp. 26–7

Tutankhaten now changed his name to Tutankhamun, 'Living Image of Amun'. There is no doubt that he and his advisers were extremely worried

about the calamitous situation in which they found themselves and used every means to propitiate the affronted gods, the results of whose anger had so reduced the country. Many monuments and fine statues were raised to the glory of the old gods, but the unfortunate boy-king's life was near its end. Like his birth, his death is subject to conjecture. It may have been natural – they were not of healthy stock – it may have been murder, though there are little signs of this; it may have been an accident; it is doubtful if the truth will ever be known. As soon as Tutankhamun was dead Ay became Pharaoh and it is to him that we owe the arrangements for the sumptuous if hasty funeral. So little time had been available that an unmatched lid was used for the sarcophagus and only the burial chamber had painted walls. The coffin was too long for the sarcophagus and had to be reduced in size, and some of the protective shrines had been put together incorrectly. None the less, in the brief time at their disposal, possibly the seventy days of embalming, the sculptors and goldsmiths of Ancient Egypt had achieved a perfection that has still to be equalled. Then there was the amazing manner in which the attendants managed to place such a vast quantity of objects into such a small space. It took Carter and his team, working with every modern device, ten years to list and remove what the robbers had left.

On the wall of the tomb behind the great sarcophagus is a painting of Ay performing the Opening of the Mouth ceremony on Tutankhamun, who is represented as Osiris. Ay is wearing the leopard skin of a setem-priest, but even at this time he may still have had some faith in Aten; he had always been a power behind the royal family and had some loyalties to the old régime. His brief reign lasted four years and his death made way for the general, Horemheb who had no relationship to this great family, the Eighteenth Dynasty, which 250 years before had cast out the Hyksos and built the greatest empire the East had ever seen. To become Pharaoh the general sought the assistance of the priests and they were glad to give it to one they saw as the restorer of the old régime. It was not long before the oracle of Amun declared him to be the son of Re and heir to the kingdom. To clinch matters Horemheb married Nefertiti's sister, Mutnedjmet who, though advanced in years, was a high priestess of Amun and this was quite sufficient to legalise the succession.

Horemheb brought enormous energy to his many tasks and quickly restored the old order, renewing the temples and the worship of the gods. He also took over the monuments, statues and temples of Tutankhamun and Ay, obliterated their names and substituted his own. In his hatred he had the beautiful city of Akhetaten at El-Amarna razed to the ground. But his efforts to banish the young king to oblivion for some reason stopped short of the destruction of his tomb. Thus after almost thirty-three centuries of darkness and silence the name Tutankhamun is known to more people today than it ever was during the lifetime of the boy-king. As the Ancient Egyptians said: 'To speak of the dead is to make them live again.'

Right: A blind harpist carved in red quartzite on a building of Queen Hatshepsut in the Temple of Karnak.

Horus: One of the very ancient gods of Egypt. Originally a sky deity he was regarded as the divine form of the king while he was alive. Subsequently he was held to be the son of Isis and Osiris, and as such he became the implacable enemy of Set as the avenger of Osiris' death. His principal shrines were at Behdet in the Delta and at Hierakonpolis and Edfu in Upper Egypt.

Overleaf: Detail of the painting on the north wall of Tutankhamun's tomb shows the king embracing Osiris while his Ka, or spiritual double, supports him from behind.

The Names of Tutankhamun

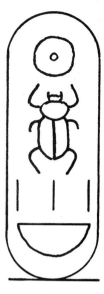

The two oval cartouches shown above contain the names by which Tutankhamun was designated most commonly on the monuments of his reign. They can be seen on many of the objects found in his tomb, carved in stone or wood, picked out in intricate inlay, even made up as elaborate and symbolic pieces of jewellery. The cartouche itself represented an oval of rope, enclosing the name; it was notionally the outline of all that the sun encircled, and stood graphically for the universal nature of the king's domain.

On the left is the more important name of the two, the prenomen or throne-name, usually preceded by the title translated as 'King of Upper and Lower Egypt'. It may be read Nebkheperure, and translated 'The Lord (or Possessor) of forms is Re', made up of the signs in the following order: ▽ =*neb* 'Lord (or Possessor)', 🪲=*kheper* 'form' (the three strokes after this sign indicate plurality and change *kheper* into *kheperu*), and ⊙ =*re* 'Re', the sun god. The signs are read in what appears to be their reverse order for reasons arising from the graphic and symbolic nature of the hieroglyphic script. Thus the name of Re is placed first because of its importance. As a whole the name declares the infinite character of the nature of the god Re, and his ability to assume a multiplicity of forms.

The second name or nomen was the king's more personal appellation, Tutankhamun. The signs may be analysed into three parts: =*tut* 'image', =*ankh* 'life' or 'live', and =*amun* 'Amun', the god. Certainty about the meaning of this name cannot be achieved because the grammatical relationships between the various parts are not clear. Among many suggestions, the most probable are 'The image of life is Amun' and 'The living image of Amun'. Again the name of the god Amun is written first in the cartouche because of its importance. This second cartouche was usually preceded by the title 'Son of Re'. The cartouche also contains three more signs, not always included, which make up an epithet much used by Tutankhamun – 'Ruler of Southern On'. The signs are =' ruler', = 'southern', and = 'On'. The great centre of sun worship in Egypt, now a part of the suburbs of Cairo, was in antiquity called On by the

TUTANKHAMUN REIGNED FROM APPROXIMATELY 1361 TO 1352 B.C. He died at about the age of nineteen and was buried in a small four-roomed tomb in the Valley of the Kings on the west bank of the Nile at Luxor. His brief reign was uneventful and had it not been for the astounding treasure found in his burial chamber the world would hardly have heard of him. The discovery of his tomb was made under such dramatic circumstances that *The Times*, London's leading newspaper, agreed to pay Lord Carnarvon the, in those days magnificent, sum of £5,000 plus three-quarters of the profits on the international sale of news, articles and pictures of the discovery. The reason for all the excitement was that not one of the royal tombs identified in the Valley of the Kings had escaped the depredations of robbers. Paintings and bas-reliefs of life in the underworld still clothed the long corridors and walls of the despoiled tombs and sometimes the plunderers had left bits of furniture or broken sarcophagi to show what might have been found. But all the treasures that the kings had hoped to provide for themselves in their future life had vanished. There remained one undiscovered tomb, that of Tutankhamun and time for the search was running out.

Permission to dig for archaeological remains in Egypt was given by the Egyptian Antiquities Service and it was from them that Lord Carnarvon, as early as 1907, had obtained his first concession. Carnarvon was not an Egyptologist but he was immensely rich. He had gone to Egypt for reasons of health in 1903 and had become interested in archaeology. He was fortunate in acquiring the services of Howard Carter who had first worked in Egypt with the famous Egyptologist, Flinders Petrie in 1892, later being employed as a skilled draughtsman by the Egypt Exploration Fund (now Society). From 1907 the two men worked together and made several important discoveries, but it was not until 1914 that the long-sought concession to dig in the Valley of the Kings was given to them and their dream of finding the tomb of Tutankhamun became a possibility. Because of the war the search was delayed until 1917 and then for five long years they excavated in vain. Finally, in what was to have been their last season and with all hope of finding the tomb vanishing, the first step that was to lead them to success appeared among the rubble.

Biban el-Moluk, or the Valley of the Kings, is a vast cul-de-sac in the tawny limestone cliffs of the Theban hills. It is an arid desolate spot where the setting sun casts long shadows and where darkness falls swiftly. In the daytime it is a heat trap, an airless stifling place where work of any kind is exhausting. It was here, except for Akhenaten, that every Pharaoh since Tuthmosis I had made his eternal home. The tombs were cut out of the cliffs – usually starting with steep steps leading down to long descending passages which finally give way to a series of rooms. Here and there false doors, deep pits and blockages made of great slabs of stone were placed to prevent the access of robbers.

Left: Tutankhamun's funeral mask, probably an exact likeness and the finest ever found in the world. It is made of solid gold inlaid with semi-precious stones. Height 54·0 cm, width 39·0 cm, depth 49·0 cm.

Overleaf: Dawn on the Nile near Luxor, little changed since the days of Tutankhamun.

Without exception all these devices failed to achieve their purpose, for the position of the tombs and their costly contents were known to a wide variety of people: priests, mourners, workmen, burial furnishers and the like, and all were plundered after the burials. Men who could excavate the huge underground chambers, some over 300 feet long with palatial rooms, could easily tunnel into the network of passages and reach the treasure. Outside the tombs lay the debris of their excavation. Like piles of broken stone at a quarry they revealed what had been going on, although even when they were removed the entrances to the tombs were still difficult to locate. Strangely enough it was this rubble that in fact protected the tomb of Tutankhamun, not indeed the rubble from his own tomb but that from the tomb of Ramesses VI which had flowed over and buried the entrance to the tomb of Tutankhamun to a great depth.

Fortunately for Carter his last efforts were spent in removing this waste material and suddenly on the morning of 4 November 1922 a stone step emerged from the mass. It was followed by fifteen others, and as they gradually came to light Carter was filled with apprehension that they might lead to an unfinished tomb but to his excitement the upper part of a blocked-up doorway was gradually revealed. It was sealed with stone and plaster. His excitement grew to fever heat, but he decided to refill the stairway and inform his patron, Lord Carnarvon, who was in England, before proceeding further. On receiving the news Lord Carnarvon set out immediately for Egypt, arriving in Luxor on 23 November with his

Below: The royal throne of Tutankhamun showing the queen anointing him under the rays of the solar disc, symbol of Aten, the sole god of the new religion introduced by Akhen-aten, the father-in-law of Tutankhamun. On this the king bears the earlier form of his name, Tutankhaten.
Right: In this funerary banquet scene three girls play music for the guests. The instruments from left to right are, a double flute, a lute and a harp. From the tomb of Nakht, scribe and astronomer. Luxor Eighteenth Dynasty, c. 1430 B.C.
Overleaf: Chair of Princess Sitamun showing her receiving gold from Nubia. She was the daughter of Amenophis III and Queen Tiye, mother of Akhenaten.

Egyptians, and Heliopolis by the Greeks; Thebes, Tutankhamun's capital, was sometimes called Southern On.

In his earliest years, during the reign of Akhenaten, and even perhaps at the outset of his own reign, Tutankhamun was called Tutankhaten. He was given his name at a time when the worship of the god Amun was proscribed, and the Aten was the sole deity worshipped by Akhenaten. In the writing of this early form of his name, the word for Aten ($\begin{smallmatrix}\end{smallmatrix}$) filled the important position which was later occupied by Amun. Several objects found in Tutankhamun's tomb bear his name in this first form.

On the spelling of the king's name in the Roman script it ought to be pointed out that no form can with certainty be said to represent precisely how it would have sounded when spoken by an Egyptian of Tutankhamun's time. The form used in this book is the one which, according to modern scholarly opinion, is likely to be closest to the original pronunciation.

The direction in which Egyptian hieroglyphics are written and the order in which the cartouches are placed depends on the way in which the scene is arranged. Any difference in the order of the cartouches in the examples shown in this book are of no consequence in the reading of the names.

We are indebted to Mr T. G. H. James for the descriptions of the Principal Deities which appear alongside the text; the Chronological Table and the notes on the names of Tutankhamun.

The sun god in the shape of a scarab being worshipped by two forms of Osiris who kneel in the sun bark travelling through the underworld at night. This is painted on the west wall of Tutankhamun's tomb.

Left: An underworld deity surrounded by a serpent holding its tail in its mouth. Detail on the side of the second shrine.

Right: Wall-painting from the tomb of Horemheb shows the general offering jars of wine to Anubis the god of embalming. Horemheb succeeded Tutankhamun and Ay as Pharaoh and restored the religion of Ancient Egypt.

Below: The Necklace of the Rising Sun, showing the sun god in the form of a scarab being worshipped by two baboons.

CHRONOLOGICAL TABLE

Including the names of the principal kings

Early Dynastic Period

First Dynasty (c. 3100–2890 B.C.)

Narmer (Menes)	Den
Aha	Semerkhet
Djer	Qaa

Second Dynasty (c. 2890–2686 B.C.)

Hotepsekhemwy	Peribsen
Nynetjer	Khasekhemwy

Old Kingdom

Third Dynasty (c. 2686–2613 B.C.)

Sanakhte	Sekhemkhet
Djoser (Zoser)	Huni

Fourth Dynasty (c. 2613–2494 B.C.)

Sneferu	Chephren
Cheops	Mycerinus

Fifth Dynasty (c. 2494–2345 B.C.)

Userkaf	Nyuserre
Sahure	Unas

Sixth Dynasty (c. 2345–2181 B.C.)

Teti	Merenre
Pepi I	Pepi II

First Intermediate Period

A time of political instability lasting from about 2181 B.C. to about 2133 B.C. including the Seventh to Tenth Dynasties, the order and names of whose kings are not fully established.

Middle Kingdom

Eleventh Dynasty (c. 2133–1991 B.C.)

Mentuhotpe I	Mentuhotpe II–IV
Inyotef I–III	

Twelfth Dynasty (c. 1991–1786 B.C.)

Ammenemes I, 1991–1962 B.C.	Sesostris III, 1878–1843 B.C.
Sesostris I, 1971–1928 B.C.	Ammenemes III, 1842–1797 B.C.

Thirteenth Dynasty (c. 1786–1633 B.C.)

Sebekhotpe III	Neferhotep

Second Intermediate Period

A further time of political instability during which Egypt was ruled in part by the Asiatic Hyksos. The Fourteenth and Sixteenth Dynasties are particularly shadowy, the former consisting of native rulers, and the latter of minor Hyksos.

Fifteenth (Hyksos) Dynasty (c. 1674–1567 B.C.)

Sheshi	Apophis I
Khyan	Apophis II

Seventeenth Dynasty (c. 1650–1567 B.C.)

Seqenenre	Kamose

New Kingdom

Eighteenth Dynasty (c. 1567–1320 B.C.)

Amosis, 1570–1546 B.C.	Tuthmosis IV, 1425–1417 B.C.
Amenophis I, 1546–1526 B.C.	Amenophis III, 1417–1379 B.C.
Tuthmosis I, 1525–1512 B.C.	Akhenaten, 1379–1362 B.C.
Tuthmosis II, 1512–1504 B.C.	Smenkhkare, 1364–1361 B.C.
Hatshepsut, 1503–1482 B.C.	Tutankhamun, 1361–1352 B.C.
Tuthmosis III, 1504–1450 B.C.	Ay, 1352–1348 B.C.
Amenophis II, 1450–1425 B.C.	Horemheb, 1348–1320 B.C.

Nineteenth Dynasty (c. 1320–1200 B.C.)

Ramesses I, 1320–1318 B.C.	Merneptah, 1236–1223 B.C.
Seti I, 1318–1304 B.C.	Amenmesses, 1222–1217 B.C.
Ramesses II, 1304–1237 B.C.	Seti II, 1216–1210 B.C.

Twentieth Dynasty (c. 1200–1085 B.C.)

Sethnakhte, 1200–1198 B.C.	Ramesses IV–XI, 1166–1085 B.C.
Ramesses III, 1198–1166 B.C.	

Late New Kingdom

From the Twenty-first to the beginning of the Twenty-fifth Dynasties (c. 1085–750 B.C.), Egypt was in political decline. The Twenty-fourth Dynasty was concurrent with the beginning of the Twenty-fifth Dynasty.

Late Period

Twenty-fifth Dynasty (c. 750–656 B.C.)

Piankhi, 750–716 B.C.	Taharqa, 689–664 B.C.
Shabaka, 716–695 B.C.	

Twenty-sixth Dynasty (c. 664–525 B.C.)

Psammetichus I, 664–610 B.C.	Apries, 589–570 B.C.
Necho II, 610–595 B.C.	Amasis, 570–526 B.C.

The Twenty-seventh Dynasty consisted of Persian conquering kings, and the Twenty-eighth–Thirtieth Dynasties of the last native Egyptian rulers. In 332 B.C. Alexander the Great conquered Egypt, and thereafter the land was ruled first by Macedonian Greeks (the Ptolemies) and then as part of the Roman Empire.

Right: A lion head made of gilded wood adorns one of the ritual beds of Tutankhamun. The eyes are made of crystal outlined in blue glass.

FURTHER READING

C. A. Aldred   *Akhenaten*. (Thames and Hudson, 1968.)
C. A. Aldred   *Jewels of the Pharaohs*. (Thames and Hudson, 1968.)
H. Carter   *The Tomb of Tutankhamen*. (In one volume paperback, Sphere Books, 1972.)
C. Desroches Noblecourt   *Tutankhamen*. (The Connoisseur and Michael Joseph, 1963;
                                    paperback Penguin Books.)
I. E. S. Edwards   *Treasures of Tutankhamun*, Catalogue of the Exhibition at the British
                                    Museum. 1972.
I. E. S. Edwards   *Introductory Guide to the Egyptian Collection at the British Museum*.
                                    (London, 1964.)
A. H. Gardiner   *Egypt of the Pharaohs*. (Oxford, 1961; also in paperback.)
T. G. H. James   *Archaeology of Ancient Egypt*. (Bodley Head, 1972.)
William MacQuitty   *Abu Simbel*. (Macdonald, 1965.)

Above: The Vulture Pendant which was round the neck of the king's mummy between the eleventh and twelfth layers of bandages. It represents the vulture goddess of Upper Egypt, Nekhbet, and was probably worn by the king during his lifetime. Maximum height 6·5 cm., maximum width 11·0 cm.